SALTWATER CROCODILES

by Katie Marsico

Children's Press®

An Imprint of Scholastic Inc.
New York   Toronto   London   Auckland   Sydney
Mexico City   New Delhi   Hong Kong
Danbury, Connecticut

Content Consultant
Dr. Stephen S. Ditchkoff
Professor of Wildlife Sciences
Auburn University
Auburn, Alabama

Photographs © 2014: age fotostock/Horizon: 15; Alamy Images:
39 (Ashley Whitworth), 19 (Dave Watts), 20 (NSP-RF), 1, 46
(Rob Walls); Bob Italiano: 44, 45 map; Dreamstime/Blagov58:
2 background, 3 background, 44 background, 45 background;
Everett Collection/Katrina Bridgeford/Rex USA: 40; Getty Images: 7
(Martin Harvey/Peter Arnold), cover (Steve Turner/Oxford Scientific);
National Geographic Stock/Wes C. Skiles: 32; Science Source: 8,
28 (ANT Photo Library), 4, 5, 27 (Jeffrey W. Lang), 24 (Michael
McCoy), 5 top, 35 (Tom McHugh); Shutterstock, Inc./Rich Lindie: 5,
36; Superstock, Inc./Reinhard Dirscherl: 16; The Image Works: 23
(Ben Copp/Auscape), 31 (Frank Woerle/Auscape), 12 (Jean-Paul
Ferrero/Auscape), 2, 3 foreground, 11 (Joan de la Malla/V&W).

Library of Congress Cataloging-in-Publication Data

Marsico, Katie, 1980–
Saltwater crocodiles / by Katie Marsico.
pages cm.—(Nature's children)
Audience: 9–12.
Audience: Grade 4 to 6.
Includes bibliographical references and index.
ISBN 978-0-531-23361-0 (lib. bdg.)
ISBN 978-0-531-25159-1 (pbk.)
1. Crocodylus porosus—Juvenile literature.
I. Title.
QL666.C925M376 2013
597.98'2—dc23   2013000094

All rights reserved. Published in 2014 by Children's Press, an imprint
of Scholastic Inc.

Printed in China 62
SCHOLASTIC, CHILDREN'S PRESS, and associated logos are
trademarks and/or registered trademarks of Scholastic Inc.

1 2 3 4 5 6 7 8 9 10 R 23 22 21 20 19 18 17 16 15 14

Saltwater Crocodiles

Class	Reptilia
Order	Crocodylia
Family	Crocodylidae
Genus	Crocodylus
Species	Crocodylus porosus
World distribution	Southeast Asia and northern Australia
Habitat	A combination of brackish, freshwater, and saltwater systems, including coastal areas and stretches of open sea
Distinctive physical characteristics	Average length of 17 feet (5.2 meters) and average weight of 1,000 pounds (450 kilograms) for adult males; excellent night and underwater vision; four short, powerful legs and a tail; 64 to 68 cone-shaped teeth up to 3 inches (7.6 centimeters) long; white or yellow underside, and brown or gray most everywhere else; streamlined body; webbed hind feet
Habits	Build nests before laying 40 to 90 eggs at a time; can swim up to 11 miles (18 kilometers) per hour in short bursts; communicate using body language and noises such as chirps, growls, barks, and hisses; hunt by silently lying in wait in the water until suitable prey passes by
Diet	Feed on anything they can overpower, including fish, turtles, lizards, snakes, crabs, birds, cattle, water buffalo, monkeys, wild boars, small sharks, and people; hatchlings feed on insects and smaller animals

Contents

CHAPTER 1

Feared and Ferocious

Flies buzz overhead as a wild boar enters a slow-moving stream in northern Australia. The boar looks around before preparing to take a drink of water. Everything seems still and safe. The animal does not suspect that danger lurks only a few feet away—or that its decision to wade into the stream will soon prove fatal.

Suddenly, 17 feet (5.2 meters) of ferocious **reptile** rips through the surface of the water. This deadly saltwater crocodile rolls from side to side as it locks the boar between its jaws and drags it downward with a mighty splash. Eventually the **prey** of the mighty **predator** drowns, and the fierce hunter slinks back into silence to enjoy its meal.

The saltwater crocodile is the largest reptile in the world. But this is not the only reason it is famous—and feared. Some saltwater crocodiles have been known to attack and eat humans!

Saltwater crocodiles often surprise their prey
by lunging suddenly out of the water.

Well-Hidden in Water

Saltwater crocodiles are also known as estuarine crocodiles, Indo-Pacific crocodiles, and salties. They get their name because they often live in **brackish environments** that contain a mixture of saltwater and freshwater. These reptiles are frequently found in **estuaries** throughout Southeast Asia and northern Australia, but people have spotted saltwater crocodiles in other settings as well. Some have even been known to swim far out to sea. They also spend time in freshwater rivers and lakes that are located farther inland from coastal areas. Such **habitats** provide saltwater crocodiles with a source of fresh drinking water.

All of these environments allow the reptiles to stay hidden as they wait for prey to approach. Like floating logs, the crocodiles simply lie motionless beneath the surface of the murky water. Eventually animals ranging from fish and crabs to sharks and water buffalo pass by. When they do, saltwater crocodiles are prepared to strike.

An unsuspecting great egret makes an easy target for a waiting saltwater crocodile.

Physical Features

Saltwater crocodiles are huge. The average length for most adult males is 17 feet (5.2 m), and they generally weigh about 1,000 pounds (450 kilograms). Males tend to be slightly larger than females. Some salties are far from average. The largest ones have measured up to 23 feet (7 m) long and weighed as much as 2,200 pounds (1,000 kg)!

Saltwater crocodiles have broad bodies with four short, powerful legs and a long tail. Their large heads feature jaws lined with 64 to 68 teeth. A pair of ridges stretches from their eyes and runs along the middle of their **snout**.

A saltwater crocodile is covered in oval-shaped scales that change color as the animals age. Young salties are light yellow with black stripes and spots. Adults have a white or yellow underside, but are brown or gray most everywhere else. Dark rings are found along their tail.

Adult male
6 ft. (1.8 m)

Saltwater crocodile
17 ft. (5.2 m)

A saltwater crocodile's coloring darkens as it ages.

CHAPTER 2

Amazing Adaptations

Saltwater crocodiles have several incredible **adaptations** that have helped them survive and become ferocious hunters. Adults face few natural enemies in the wild. However, buffalo sometimes destroy the areas where the crocodiles nest. In addition, water pythons, monitor lizards, large birds, and other crocodiles are often a threat to younger salties. But for the most part, fully grown saltwater crocodiles do not fear predators.

On the other hand, these reptiles hunt a wide variety of prey. Most saltwater crocodiles will feed on anything they can attack and kill. This includes fish, turtles, lizards, snakes, and crabs. Birds, cattle, water buffalo, monkeys, wild boars, small sharks, and people are also among the victims that have been known to fill a saltwater crocodile's belly. Younger crocodiles eat insects and smaller animals until they are ready to take down larger prey.

Fish are no match for a hungry saltwater crocodile.

A Lethal Bite

One adaptation that has allowed saltwater crocodiles to climb to the top of the food chain is their jaws. These reptiles are able to exert more than 3,700 pounds (1,678 kg) of force when they clamp down on prey with their teeth. A saltwater crocodile relies on this jaw strength to drag its victims into the water and prevent them from escaping. It also uses its mouth to grab and hang on to larger animals such as water buffalo.

A saltwater crocodile's teeth measure up to 3 inches (7.6 centimeters) long. When the reptile shuts its mouth, the cone-shaped teeth lock together like the hooks on a steel trap. This makes it difficult for prey to escape the crocodile's deadly bite. The size and sharpness of its teeth also help the crocodile tear off chunks of its victim's flesh.

FUN FACT! Scientists believe that a saltie can bite with about the same force as a *T. rex* could.

Saltwater crocodiles have the strongest bite of any animal in the world today.

A Predator's Powerful Moves

Remarkably strong muscles line a saltwater crocodile's legs, midsection, and tail. These muscles allow the crocodile to swim long distances at sea. They also help the reptile lunge at prey and carry out a movement known as the death roll. During the death roll, a saltwater crocodile rolls over and over in the water while holding prey in its mouth. This upsets the victim's sense of balance and often causes the unlucky animal to drown.

In addition, a saltwater crocodile's muscles give it the ability to reach high speeds during short bursts of movement. These reptiles have been known to swim up to 11 miles (18 kilometers) per hour, which is faster than an Olympic swimmer at top speed. However, they are not able to move this fast over long distances. A crocodile's **streamlined** body cuts down water resistance, which boosts its speed. Another way saltwater crocodiles increase their swimming speed is by whipping their tail back and forth in the water. Finally, a saltwater crocodile's webbed hind feet allow it to make fast turns while swimming.

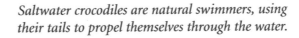

Saltwater crocodiles are natural swimmers, using their tails to propel themselves through the water.

Spectacular Scales

A saltwater crocodile's tough, bony scales provide protection. In addition, the grayish-green coloring of the scales helps the animal to blend in with its surroundings.

But how do saltwater crocodiles stay warm when they have scales instead of fur or feathers? Like all reptiles, they are **cold-blooded**. Luckily, saltwater crocodiles have adaptations that help them control their body temperature.

Blood vessels in the skin help them absorb the warmth of the sun. To cool down, saltwater crocodiles head to the water or shady areas on land. They also open their gigantic jaws to release extra body heat through the damp skin on their mouth and tongue.

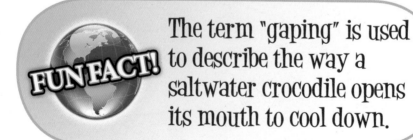

FUN FACT! The term "gaping" is used to describe the way a saltwater crocodile opens its mouth to cool down.

While it might look like saltwater crocodiles are simply being lazy when they lay in the sunlight, they are actually performing the important task of keeping their body temperature at a healthy level.

Sight, Sound, and Smell

A saltwater crocodile's eyes are protected by three pairs of eyelids. One set is **transparent** and allows the reptile to see beneath the water's surface. Most experts agree that saltwater crocodiles have excellent eyesight. Their eyes let in more light than humans' eyes do. As a result, it is likely that saltwater crocodiles have better night vision than people.

These reptiles also have a sharp sense of hearing. Slits along the side of a saltwater crocodile's head are connected to its inner ears. The slits close when the animal moves underwater.

A saltwater crocodile's nostrils are located along the top of its snout. This lets the reptile detect scents in the air even when the rest of its body is hidden beneath the surface of the water. Special flaps of tissue on its nostrils and behind its tongue stop water from entering its lungs.

A saltwater crocodile's eyes, ears, and nostrils often remain above the water even when the rest of its body is submerged.

The Belly of the Beast

Saltwater crocodiles use a wide variety of adaptations to hunt and kill prey. Yet they also depend on their physical features to digest their food. For starters, their trachea, or windpipe, is long and flexible. This allows them to squeeze large meals down their throats whole.

In addition, a saltwater crocodile's heart has an extra artery, or blood vessel. Scientists suspect that this artery carries blood to the crocodile's stomach. Certain acids in the blood help break down hard matter such as bones.

A saltwater crocodile also has a slow **metabolism**. This means that it does not need to eat every day to survive. As a result, it can live off a single meal for quite a long time. Experts say this is how some saltwater crocodiles have survived for more than a year without feeding!

A large meal, such as this wild pig, can keep a saltwater crocodile satisfied for a long time.

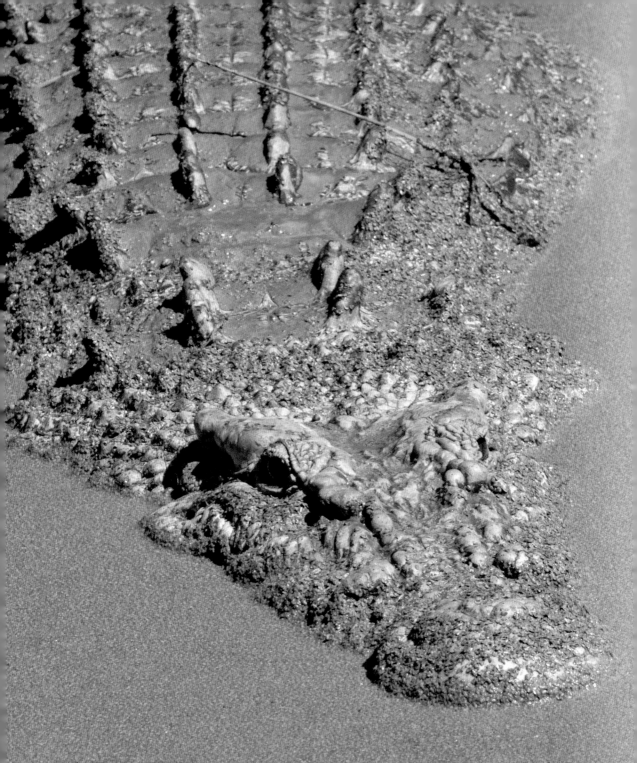

Healthy Bodies, Big Brains

Saltwater crocodiles are extremely hardy animals. They are very fast to recover from injuries. This is amazing considering the high levels of bacteria that fill the water where they spend so much time. A saltwater crocodile has a strong immune system that allows it to easily fight off infections and diseases. Not many other reptiles possess this important adaptation.

In addition, few have such a complex brain. A crocodile's brain features an outer layer called a cerebral cortex that is missing in most reptiles. This layer controls various sensations and processes such as thought and memory. Scientists say the cerebral cortex gives crocodiles an edge over their reptile relatives when it comes to brainpower.

Bacteria-filled water can make many animals sick, but a saltwater crocodile's strong immune system helps protect it.

CHAPTER 3

A Saltie's Life Cycle

A saltwater crocodile can live for a very long time compared to most other animals. Some have been known to survive for up to 70 years in the wild. Throughout this long lifetime, a saltwater crocodile does not spend much time with other crocodiles.

Saltwater crocodiles are extremely **territorial**. Males often fight each other for control of areas where they hope to hunt or **mate**. They also prove their **dominance**, defend territory, and attract mates by making noises to communicate. Saltwater crocodiles "talk" to one another by forcing air through their vocal boxes. Such sounds—and the vibrations they cause in the water—send messages to nearby crocodiles. Most crocodile calls take the form of chirps, growls, barks, and hisses. A saltwater crocodile also relies on body language to communicate. It raises its head and swings its tail to deliver various social signals.

Saltwater crocodiles make threatening noises to defend their territory, especially when they are guarding a nest of eggs.

Ready to Reproduce

Saltwater crocodiles come together to mate each year during the wet season. This is when the areas where they live receive large amounts of rainfall. The wet season varies by location.

During this time, male saltwater crocodiles usually head to freshwater river systems. Once they claim a mating ground, they defend it against other males. Then they make long, low growls and use body language to attract females to their territory. Male saltwater crocodiles, or bulls, are first ready to mate when they are about 16 years old. Females, or cows, often start mating between the ages of 10 and 12.

A female saltwater crocodile prepares to lay her eggs by building a nest that is made out of plants and mud. She uses her hind legs to shape the nest so that it is raised off the ground. This is especially important because heavy rains can flood low-lying areas during the wet season.

Saltwater crocodile mothers build their huge mound nests
so that their eggs will be above the level of rising waters.

After the Eggs Hatch

A female saltwater crocodile lays between 40 and 90 eggs. She then covers her nest with plant matter and dirt and keeps a careful watch over it. It takes about 90 days for the babies—which are called hatchlings or crocklets—to fully develop and push through the eggshells. The female digs away the layer of mud and leaves covering the nest when she hears a chirping sound. This is the noise the crocklets make shortly after they hatch. The babies weigh just 2 to 2.5 ounces (57 to 71 grams) when they are born!

Mother saltwater crocodiles stay close to their young for about eight months. During this time, the hatchlings live in groups called crèches. Adult saltwater crocodiles protect the babies while they learn how to swim and hunt.

FUN FACT! A mother crocodile carries her crocklets in her mouth until they are ready to move through the water on their own.

The temperature of a saltwater crocodile's nest determines whether the crocklets are male or female.

CHAPTER 4

From Past to Present

Saltwater crocodiles have had a long time to adapt to the world around them and develop into powerful predators. Their earliest ancestors walked the earth alongside dinosaurs. People have discovered crocodile fossils that date back 240 million years!

Experts believe that these ancient animals looked much like today's crocodiles. Fossils show that they had narrow skulls, pointed snouts, and similar bone structures in their jaws and ankles. Yet prehistoric crocodiles were a lot bigger than their modern relatives. Some species measured up to 50 feet (15 m) long!

Scientists first recognized saltwater crocodiles as a species of crocodile in 1801. The species' scientific name is *Crocodylus porosus* and has Greek and Latin roots. The word *Crocodylus* means "pebble worm" and refers to a saltwater crocodile's long body, bumpy scales, and grayish-brown coloring. The term *porosus* is defined as "full of calluses." A callus is a thickened layer of skin. *Porosus* describes the rough, lumpy skin on top of a saltwater crocodile's snout.

Scientists carefully remove layers of dirt from fossils to reveal the important details beneath.

Incredible Crocodilians

Like all crocodiles, saltwater crocodiles belong to an **order** known as crocodilians. Reptiles such as alligators, caimans, and gharials are also grouped in this category. Crocodilians have long jaws, short legs, and a powerful tail. Saltwater crocodiles are the largest crocodilians.

At first, some people mistook saltwater crocodiles for alligators. This is because, like alligators, they have a broader body than most crocodiles. Salties also have a longer snout than many of their closest relatives.

Scientists also tell crocodiles apart by studying their scutes. A scute is a thin, flat piece of bone that is located under an animal's scales. Most crocodilians have scutes on their neck but saltwater crocodiles lack these scutes. In addition, a saltwater crocodile's scutes are generally smaller than those of other crocodile species.

FUN FACT! A crocodile's scales help it sense small changes in water pressure, such as those caused by splashes on the surface.

Scutes form ridged lines down a saltwater crocodile's back and tail.

A Glimpse at Gharials

Gharials are close relatives of saltwater crocodiles. These large, fish-eating crocodiles measure between 12 and 16 feet (3.7 and 4.9 m) long and can sometimes weigh up to 2,200 pounds (1,000 kg). Gharials are found mainly in the freshwater river systems of India and Nepal in southern Asia.

Unlike saltwater crocodiles, gharials are not known for attacking and eating humans. They also do not have the jaw strength to catch and kill large prey. In addition, their bodies are more cylinder-shaped than those of saltwater crocodiles.

Scientists consider gharials to be critically endangered. This means that they face an extremely high risk of being completely wiped off the planet. Habitat destruction and other human activity have had a damaging effect on the gharial population.

Gharials have much narrower snouts than crocodiles or alligators.

CHAPTER 5

Altering Human Attitudes

Experts suspect that between 200,000 and 300,000 saltwater crocodiles roam the earth today. Scientists do not believe that these remarkable reptiles are likely to become endangered anytime soon. Nevertheless, their long-term future remains uncertain if people's attitudes toward them do not change.

It is true that saltwater crocodiles have been responsible for injuring and killing human beings. But many of the tragedies involving saltwater crocodiles could be avoided. People often do not pay enough attention to warning signs that alert the public when crocodiles have been spotted in a certain area. Others incorrectly assume that they will never be caught off guard and attacked. Such assumptions are foolish and have cost people their lives.

Fear frequently drives people to hate these truly amazing animals. Some experts suspect that growing numbers of saltwater crocodiles are being killed as a result of terror and misunderstanding.

It is extremely important to obey signs warning
swimmers about saltwater crocodiles.

Kakadu National
Park

A Look at the
Long-Term Future

Saltwater crocodiles have other reasons to fear humans as well. People hunt these animals for their meat and skin. Saltwater crocodile leather is considered quite valuable. In addition, the development of human settlements in wetland areas poses a possible threat to crocodile populations in the long term.

Many people are in favor of working with conservationists to raise public awareness about saltwater crocodiles. Some support farms where the reptiles are raised for their meat and skin in a controlled environment. These people believe that this is less cruel than illegal hunting and that it provides an opportunity to promote education about saltwater crocodiles.

There is good reason for human beings to fear this species. However, they need to balance their uncertainty over saltwater crocodiles with a sense of respect. These animals may seem like terrifying monsters, but they are also remarkable predators who deserve to rule the wild world around them for centuries to come.

Special cruises offer tourists the opportunity to safely view wild saltwater crocodiles.

Words to Know

adaptations (ad-ap-TAY-shuhnz) — changes in animals or plants that help them fit better in their environment

ancestors (AN-ses-turz) — ancient animal species that are related to modern species

brackish (BRAK-ish) — somewhat salty

cold-blooded (KOHLD BLUHD-id) — having a body temperature that changes according to the temperature of the surroundings

conservationists (kon-sur-VAY-shun-ists) — people who work to protect an environment and the living things in it

dominance (DAH-muh-nuntz) — the power of one animal or person to assert its will over another

environments (en-VYE-ruhn-muhnts) — the natural surroundings of living things, such as the air, land, or sea

estuaries (ES-choo-er-eez) — the wide parts of rivers, where they join oceans

fossils (FAH-suhlz) — bones, shells, or other traces of an animal or plant from long ago, preserved as rock

habitats (HAB-uh-tats) — places where an animal or a plant naturally lives

hardy (HAHR-dee) — strong, healthy, and able to survive in difficult conditions

mate (MATE) — to join together to produce babies

metabolism (muh-TAB-uh-liz-uhm) — the rate at which an animal uses energy

order (OR-dur) — a group of related plants or animals that is bigger than a family but smaller than a class

predator (PRED-uh-tur) — an animal that lives by hunting other animals for food

prey (PRAY) — an animal that is hunted by another animal for food

reptile (REP-tile) — a cold-blooded animal that has a backbone, can breathe on land, and often has scales and lays eggs

snout (SNOUT) — the long front part of an animal's head that includes the nose, mouth, and jaws

species (SPEE-sheez) — one of the groups into which animals and plants of the same genus are divided; members of the same species can mate and have offspring

streamlined (STREEM-lined) — designed or shaped to minimize resistance to air or water

territorial (ter-uh-TOR-ee-uhl) — defensive of a certain area

transparent (trans-PAIR-uhnt) — clear like glass so that objects on the other side can be seen clearly

Habitat Map

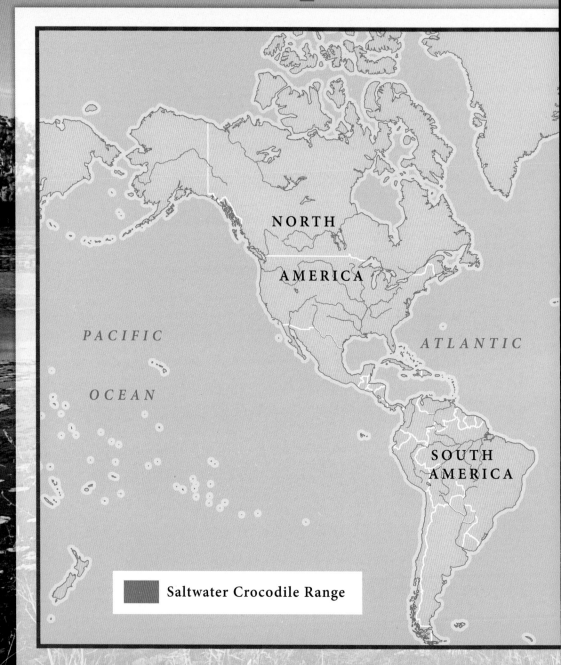

NORTH
AMERICA

PACIFIC

OCEAN

ATLANTIC

SOUTH
AMERICA

Saltwater Crocodile Range

ARCTIC OCEAN

EUROPE

ASIA

PACIFIC

OCEAN

AFRICA

OCEAN

INDIAN

OCEAN

AUSTRALIA

Find Out More

Books

Gibbs, Maddie. *Crocodiles*. New York: PowerKids Press, 2011.

Saia, Stephanie. *Hunting With Crocodiles*. New York: Gareth Stevens, 2012.

Sexton, Colleen. *The Saltwater Crocodile*. Minneapolis: Bellwether Media, 2012.

Visit this Scholastic Web site for more
information on saltwater crocodiles:
www.factsfornow.scholastic.com
Enter the keywords **Saltwater Crocodiles**

Index

Page numbers in *italics* indicate a photograph or map.

About the Author

Katie Marsico is the author of more than 100 children's books. She enjoyed learning about saltwater crocodiles—though she's not sure if she'd ever want to see one up close. She dedicates this book to Russell Primm and his wonderful and talented staff at Editorial Directions.